EBAY SELLING

SIMPLIFIED

Author: George Pain

TABLE OF CONTENTS

DISCLAIMER

ABOUT THE AUTHOR

George Pain is an entrepreneur, author and business consultant. He specializes in setting up online businesses from scratch, investment income strategies and global mobility solutions. He has built several businesses from the ground up, and is excited to share his knowledge with readers. Here is a list of his books.

Books of George Pain

INTRODUCTION TO SELLING ON EBAY

Need To Know Economy Basics

The eBay Market is a giant auction else but it is own economy because many of the items that are sold on the eBay website make up the majority of what's sold in a country. Beyond things like food or alcohol or anything perishable really, most of the products that you find on eBay will be something that you can find at a certain type of store in that country.

This means that the eBay website is its own economy and understanding basic economic principles is how you can, generally, sell most of your products. There are some eBay accounts that actually have advertisers and marketing teams in order to sell on eBay, but there are also individuals who are making a quick buck on eBay by selling their own products in a much smaller quantity. The economic principles are actually really simple and if you just take the time to understand it then you will find that it will help you out in the long run.

Most of the basics revolve around something called supply and demand, which means that every product has a certain available supply and requested demand. In order to maximize sales, you have to find the middle point where there is enough supply of something to meet the demand of something but no more than that because then you have an excess in supply.

Check for Scarcity

Scarcity is often the best form of selling any type of product that you can get out on the market. This doesn't always mean that you will be the only one that has the product to sell, but it does mean that there are lower amounts of competition. The problem with scarcity is that you can have too much of the scarcity as well as too little of the scarcity. If a market has too little of a scarcity it usually means that the product doesn't sell very well and the competitors that you might go up against are only selling the product because they are new to the market or that is the only product that they have to sell.

Scarcity refers to the amount of product in circulation of sales and determining whether a product has a usable sense of scarcity also determines how much of the item you can sell at one given time. If a product is really popular but the scarcity for the product is really high, then the return rate of the product that you are selling, that has the scarcity, will also be rather high because customers will be willing to pay more for it as they find it harder to find.

The first problem that you encounter with scarcity is the fact that it is scarce and this means that it will be a problem for you to locate and sell on a regular basis. Unless the return rate is over 25%, then selling an item that is exceedingly scarce is a bad idea if you plan to run an eBay business. The reason for this is that even though a popular product may be scarce and the return rate may be high, that doesn't mean that you will be able to consistently find a producer of that item. This means that the product wouldn't be sustainable for a long period of time.

The second problem with scarcity is that you may find yourself dealing with illegal individuals. A case in point is the USB drive market, which is absolutely huge but most people know not to buy USB drives from China and this is because those individuals have found tricks to increase the drive capacity that's being read from the computer so that it seems like they're selling a more expensive product than they are. This is also a problem with a lot of products that are technology-based that come from Asian cultures because those areas tend to sell products that are false. That doesn't mean that all products coming from that area are bad, it just means that there are a lot of people in that market that have no problem with ripping off their customers. If you are a new seller to this market, then being able to sell such a drive would depend on factors like living in the United States of America or United Kingdom because those are notably trustworthy areas when it comes to selling technology.

An example of this is the false CPU and GPU markets that have exploded in the past few years. Repair companies tend to go to eBay for most of their repair products and one of the most common repair products that people want is a GPU or CPU from a laptop. These companies fraudulently make older CPUs seem like newer CPUs. Therefore, unless the seller has a high reputation for delivering the product that the repairperson wants, the product is normally not sold. The worst part about this is that these products tend to be sold in a bulk fashion, which means that when the repairperson goes to buy this product, the product is worth hundreds to even thousands of dollars and they may get a product that's completely useless. This is why you have to be careful about which markets you enter.

Check for Sustainability

Another thing that you want to check for is the sustainability of a current market because unless you can consistently make money from the market, then you're not going to be able to constantly be looking for that same type of product and optimizing for the sales of that product. When I talk about sustainability, I talk about being able to sell a certain product on a consistent basis. There are two different types of sustainability and one of them is better than the other because of reliability.

The first type of sustainability is buying in bulk and then selling individually because most people don't want to buy in bulk. Let's go back to the CPU and GPU product that I was talking about before. The CPU for a certain laptop could be anywhere from $30 to $90 and much more for a singular CPU. However, at bulk price, you could easily get somewhere around a hundred of these CPUs for $10,000-$50,000. This means you could potentially get somewhere close to $30,000 to $80,000 in profit because you managed to buy a sellable product in bulk. This would be sustainable because you have a hundred of these CPUs and you don't need to look anywhere else in order to make this type of sale. Most people don't want to do this type of investment unless they're already big at selling on eBay because it does tend to take a large investment to begin selling singular items from bulk items, but it is one of the best forms of sustainability because you can stock up on it for a long period of time. The only problem with this type of sustainability, especially if we're talking about the CPU, is whether your product will be outdated by the time you sell everything.

The second type of sustainability comes from being a middleman to services outside of your area that are not marketed online. An example of this is if you have phone screens from China and you have a seller inside of China that's willing to ship you certain types of phone screens for certain prices. Normally, these phone screens can be anywhere from $5 to $50 and more depending on the model of the phone that you're asking for and how rare it is or how new it is. You could easily turn around and make a profit of anywhere from $5 to $50 and more in your own country because of price differences and local availability. The problem with this is that your supplier may not always have a consistent supply of a certain type of product or may be able to sell it to a different individual before you finally make a sale on that product once you have listed it. This type of issue means that you could easily lose profit by having to immediately buy a smartphone screen from another eBay seller in order to get that product to the customer's door.

Check for Quality Standards

One of the things that you must do as an eBay seller is to quality inspect the products that you're actually selling and the supplier that you're getting them from. What this means is that you need to buy a product or have them ship your product so that you can see what type of product you are selling. This will give you a range of customers you can sell to because you can't sell a new product if the product that you get has some wear and tear on it. Additionally, some of the products that you buy or inspect will be outdated and won't be something that will sell on eBay so you do need to account for the potential that a product that you want to get because it's extremely cheap won't be able to sell on eBay because no one is currently using that product.

Outdated

One of the most frustrating things that you can deal with as an eBay seller is not being able to sell enough of a product before it becomes outdated. Once something becomes outdated, it becomes extremely hard to sell that product because no one wants it anymore. Additionally, just because something becomes outdated doesn't mean it's unsellable, but it does mean that you will likely have to take a harder hit in profits. An example of this is whenever a new GPU comes out, the previous GPU usually goes down by around a $100 to $200. This means that you could potentially take a loss if you see a GPU coming out and you only have the previous GPU in your arsenal. In addition, the reason why you see me talking about technology a lot is because it is one of the most commonly repaired items and, thus, one of the most valuable markets to get into.

Wear and Tear

Almost all products will have a certain amount of wear and tear to them depending on how used they were, but understanding just how much an item is worn is essential to selling it on eBay. A person will only accept a phone that has a minor scratch on it if it is in fact only a minor scratch because, otherwise, they will come after you for a discounted price if they get a phone that has a large gash on it. This is understandable, because you wouldn't want something that was originally touted as being a near-perfect phone versus a phone that looked like it had been run over with a car. Therefore, understanding the range at which your product will have wear and tear on it is extremely important because it not only affects your sale price but it also affects your reputation on eBay and reputation is almost everything you have to sell a product on eBay.

Acceptable Minimums

Each market will have acceptable minimums on what you can say is wear and tear and what you can say is just for parts only because there's a certain level of acceptability among consumers when they're dealing with a product. A great example of this is the solar cell market that has recently exploded in the past few years. Due to the price of new solar cells, many people have turned to buying broken solar cells but they only want to buy solar cells that will provide them with a price discount when they compare them to the new solar cells that are out on the market. This means that you need to test the power limits of the solar cell that you are selling them in order to understand whether it fits the acceptable minimum set by the eBay market or not. Each market will have different acceptable minimums, which is why you need to know your market very well before you decide to go into any market.

Check for Regulations

EBay is really fickle about the laws that it will take on but most of the time you are on your own if you decide to sell a certain product on their website. Most of the sellers take full responsibility for any legalities that they might have in terms of their own products. This is why it's really important to know of any regulations in countries that you want to be selling in. EBay has several different sister locations or websites that sell to countries like Germany and Australia, and understanding that there are products that you can't sell in those areas is really important to not only keeping your account but also staying out of that country's jail.

A great example of this is selling a product in Canada. Baby walkers, something that is commonly used in the United States to help babies begin to walk in the early years, are actually banned in Canada and can result in a fine of $100,000 or six months of jail time if you try to sell it. There are a lot of these different laws in other countries and most of them come with very heavy fines and, most of the time you, just can't claim ignorance of the law when you sell a product in that country. Additionally, places like Germany, where you can sell online, make you a sort of temporary citizen when you sell in their markets. This means that the laws that normally apply to their own citizens can apply to you in the online space and if you try to sell something controversial, because it makes a lot of money in that online space, then you might have to face the legality laws behind that.

On top of this, there are certain items that are you are not allowed to buy or sell on eBay because of regulations by eBay. For instance, anything dealing with a beverage container that contains alcohol or anything that's considered a replica of another item cannot be sold on eBay regardless of how popular the original item is or how popular the alcohol that you are selling is or how stringent your parameters are for selling that alcohol. An example of this issue that would be affecting you or me, because one of the popular markets is technology, would be the fact that you are, generally, not allowed to sell any type of tobacco products on eBay. The reason why this might affect us is that one of the technologies that is really popular is the e-cigarette market and the United States just passed a regulation that forces e-cigarettes to be treated as tobacco products. This could mean that, overtime; eBay will remove any of the listing for repair parts on e-cigarette products and the replacement parts for many of the secondary devices that go along with e-cigarettes such as RBAs (ReBuildable Atomizer). Understanding the regulations of a country is really important to knowing what you can and cannot sell, which is why you need to know that beforehand before you go into a market.

Different eBay Markets Want Different Items

It's important to keep an eye on which markets you want to sell to because some markets do well with certain items than others. For instance, the US market tends to do really well with necklaces and pendants while the German market does really well with PC and console video games. This primarily has to do with different cultural needs in America, one of the most common things to date is to give others necklaces and pendants or to buy them for yourself. America has one of the largest communities you can sell to in terms of jewelry and this is because not only is it popular among America women, transgender, and gay people, but you also have the fact that most of the men tend to gift their women in jewelry. On the other hand, Germany is more about technology advancements when it comes to the online market. That isn't to say that Germany doesn't have an equal amount of necklace and pendant buying customers, it just means that you tend to have more sale rates with PC and console games rather than necklace and pendants.

This is extremely important when you're dealing with certain types of sales, especially if you're going to go ahead and go into the popular market of repair parts. Almost the entirety of Asia is immune to sales for technology because most of Asia is where technology is produced. This means that Asia is the number one country for repair parts most of the time. Therefore, trying to sell something like a motherboard or CPUs to this continent will likely result in failure while buying it and selling it to a country where many people tend to break their own devices, the United States of America, would end up in a success rather than a failure. This is because different countries have different priorities to them and it's very important to test your waters if you don't have the data in front of you already.

Most of the time, you can usually find out which countries will want which items by simply searching for it in Google. The most common way to search for what is sold on eBay that is popular in a country is to simply search on Google the country along with "most purchased item" or "items." Another, less predictable way, is to find out which industries made money in the past, because normally accessories or repair parts that can go with that industry do very well in the following year. The honest truth is that many people break items that are new to their environment because they're new to them.

BEST ITEMS TO SELL ON EBAY

Rare Books

Rare books are a great category to sell from because it requires very little investment with a lot of potential to begin understanding and how you can sell products inside of the eBay Market. Most rare booksellers will take a scanner to them to rummages, yard sales, and even Goodwill or other thrift stores in order to see the price of a book online. Since they can automatically look up the price, they can figure out whether the book is worth selling or not based on what the prices online. Additionally, most of them don't even need to buy a scanner and they just need to buy an application to go on their phone that does this for them.

However, once again we have the issue of the newer the item is then the more it is worth and if you're buying something at a rummage sale or Goodwill then you can't expect the product to look absolutely pristine. Additionally, you have to think about how much the shipping for that book costs because some books are quite heavy and aren't worth the profit margin that you would gain from selling them.

Very rarely are you going to make a lot of money doing this but it is a great staple if you want to begin making a good reputation for yourself on eBay as well as a decent bit of money doing it. There are some people that live in cities that are big enough for them to just go around the day and find rare books; but most people don't live in those types of cities, which makes this form of eBay selling unsustainable.

Repair Parts

I've talked a lot about how repair parts make up a general amount of the eBay market and while that this is true to most of what I do, that doesn't mean it'll be true for you. The repair part market is excellent because you can usually find a wholesaler to provide you with a large quantity of a particularly hot item used in repairs for relatively cheap by going over to a different countries website. The reason why this is popular for me is that I understand Mandarin, which means that I can go to their websites in China and find the websites that sell CPUs and GPUs in bulk for relatively cheap along with many other different parts.

The ability to understand a language where you can get a cheaper deal (because of the knowledge) is essential to many of the markets that you'll be dealing with. Those who are in Asia understand that the American population that sell repair parts on eBay look for bulk products so that they can sell them singularly. By knowing that I can read Mandarin, I can avoid being marketed to as though I am an American but rather that I am native to China. Since repair companies are also in China, they do tend to buy the same products but, because they are Chinese, the sellers of the product can't charge a high price as they would to an American. This means that I would save a lot of money by going over to a Chinese website to buy in bulk because I would be buying the price that natives would be buying at rather than the price that I would be buying it from an American standpoint. Additionally, if I were to buy cheap bulk brands in the English language then I wouldn't be able to sell that product singularly because it's in

English and my buyers are probably going to be English speakers, which means they can easily find this same resource that I did.

However, while I may be talking about CPUs and GPUs, the remainder of the PC is a very common market but it's not as common as the CPUs and the GPS. There are many motherboards that can you utilize several different types of CPUs but there is only one motherboard that can be replaced by another motherboard and unless that technology is still current then I am not likely to sell it very quickly. The best part about this type of buy and sell product is the fact that I can usually save money by transferring currencies because the dollar is not the same value as the money used by the Chinese. In fact, there are only a few currencies in the world that are still above the American dollar and this allows me to save money via the conversion rate. This last trick is actually something people use a lot in order to make significant amounts of money. All that a person has to do is manage to get money via labor in that currency and then trade to American dollars in order to make money like that. However, the more common way to do this is to live in a country that has a very low

20

currency value and then work for American dollars in order to convert the American dollars into the cheaper currency and thus giving that individual much more of the currency than they would normally get for the work that they did.

Limited Products and Collectables

This market is a market where you are likely going to be the hated individual in your local area, primarily by many of those who wait on the product that you buy out at the store. Companies will often release a limited product or a collectible for a certain amount of time and these people will use all of their money to purchase the entire stock of product so that no one else can get it. Great examples of this are the people who buy out the peppermint Suave shampoo at my local store. Since a lot of people tend to like this type of shampoo and it is often good for people who can't deal with intense smells, it sells rather fast and by paying attention to this fact the good people who do sales in limited products and collectibles have found a niche market where they can sell quite a bit. Each bottle normally costs somewhere around $3 to $4, but once the bulk buyer has managed to get their hands on it, you can usually find it on the eBay market for a severely high price markup. For instance, the peppermint shampoo normally sells for $15 a bottle on eBay. Subtract the $2 to $4 that it requires to ship this item and you have a potential profit of $7 per bottle and you can usually buy somewhere around 20 bottles, which makes for a great sale, especially if you can get much more than that.

The main problem with the limited products market is that it is in fact limited even though you can buy huge amounts in the beginning. There's also a secondary problem with limited products because they're not always popular and the only way that you know that there is a popular limited product is if you find it difficult to buy them in the first place. These products don't have an annual sales report that you can follow or a trend on Twitter that you can follow, you just have to keep an eye out for limited products being sold in popular stores that keep on being sold out. Then, once you find this product, you have to keep up with the demand of the product so you have to buy all of the stuff from the market in order to sell it at a higher price in the eBay market and then deal with angry customers who want more of it because it was a limited item. This makes the market incredibly competitive and difficult to stay inside of because of how often you have to keep an eye on the products that may or may not sell very well. Since companies tend to come out with limited items quite often, this means that you might as well run a 24-hour clock to see which products that are limited provide the best sales or are being sold out the fastest. It's a very competitive market to get into and only one where the sale is nearly triple to quadruple the size of normal return but this comes with the obvious sacrifice of not being able to invest into many other markets.

Discontinued Movies

Discontinued movies are often very similar to limited editions, but they are not classified as limited editions because they were once limitless. In fact, this means that you can often go to garage sales or rummages to find exceedingly expensive VHS tapes that are no longer sold such as the Prince of Egypt. These exceedingly rare VHS tapes can range anywhere from an additional $10 to even a couple hundred dollars, and, lastly, to even a couple thousand dollars depending on if the tape was controversial enough. There are some movies that are still controversial and banned in certain countries, but this can usually be found out by using a simple and quick Google search. This is also one of those markets where the new product tends to sell better than the used product because there are a number of collectors who only collect old VHS tapes that are no longer sold that are really hard to find in pristine condition. Examples of this are the Disney films that no longer have certain features in them that became controversial once the internet was born. A great example of this is the priest inside of The Little Mermaid that has a little bump where the priest's penis would be. This tape normally runs within the hundreds of dollars because the rather creepy society of the internet wants the documented proof that this still existed back on VHS.

Any movie that has ever been modified in order to be sold to the general public will have a certain edition out in the public that's worth buying because of the modification. The lack of modification makes the product more expensive because most modifications only happen a short time after the movie has already been released and most movie producers will request for the movie to be returned only to find out that

24

very little people even bother to return the videos in the first place. However, that does mean that the movie producer decided to stop selling the unmodified version and the unmodified version becomes a limited edition of the movie with a relatively small seller base that is likely not even looking to sell the movie.

The obvious problem with this market is that it's not very sustainable since you can only find one or two good movies within a rummage pile. The odds of you finding a collection of multiple movies that will sell twice is relatively low and trying to invest in such a technique for selling on eBay may work for certain individuals, but most individuals tend to want profits to roll in on a consistent basis.

Restricted Technology

This is an area that's really difficult to work in because you have to be careful about what technologies you can and cannot sell. For instance, it is a federal crime to sell any type of Radio Frequency Jammer because it could affect with government business in America. However, restricted technology does not necessarily mean that it is a technology that is banned. An example of this is the fact that there are some smartphones that are not purchasable inside of the United States. Just as well, there are also some smartphone technologies that are not accessible outside of a certain cell phone company's paid plan. These are situations where the individual wants the device but doesn't want the tentacles that tend to come attached to it.

An example of this was when I first bought my Samsung Galaxy phone off of eBay, which was previously unlocked for me by someone who owned the eBay account. Instead of buying a phone on the official website of my cell phone company's plans, I decided to "bring my own device" and this device was the Samsung Galaxy phone that I made the purchased for $45 that was unlocked. This is significantly less in comparison to what the official site would have had me pay for it and this is a form of restricted technology.

The term restricted means that there are circumstances that prevent many users from being able to get their hands on something outside of those conditions. This market includes unlocked cell phones, some technology that's no longer sold by a company and cannot be backed by a company anymore, and a lot of other different items that aren't actually illegal. This area is popular because it usually represents a much cheaper market. Going back to my example of my Samsung Galaxy phone, I saved around $300 by going on eBay and purchasing my own phone that was unlocked from the company of wherever they got it from. This is where the value of the market lies because you can normally get unlocked phones out of Asia really easily. The only problem with smartphones coming out of Asia is that there are a ton of companies that will use older models of phones and place newer operating systems on it. A worst-case example of this is the common iPhone market where the seller will take an old Android phone and put on a iPhone "likeness" operating system in order to sell the phone. Once you get the phone, it becomes quite obvious that you just got sold an Android with a system that looks like the official iPhone operating system but has some serious features that are lacking.

Fitness Trackers

Fitness trackers are another area that's a little gray because some of the sellers are just people who've managed to get a deal on the fitness tracker but there are also a lot of individuals who are selling knock-off trackers. Right now, the fitness tracker is a compulsive buy more than anything else except for a few individuals who need to make sure they monitor how much they walk a day. If you're a person who constantly looks for the deals that companies give out then you might know of some place like Brad's Deals or Massdrop, which are two popular websites to become acquainted with if you want to get prices lower than what you find at the retail store for brand name products. An example of this is the Fitbit that sits on my arm. Normally, this Fitbit would sell for nearly $100 but, because I got it on Massdrop, I only paid $45. I could have easily ordered the maximum amount allowed and then sold each of them for double the price that I paid for it because the buyers on eBay might be ignorant of such locations on the internet.

On the other hand, there are a lot of knock-off companies that will sell this type of product for much cheaper and this, once again, shows that is almost always best to know a location that sells knock-off products for cheap prices. There is a difference between a knockoff product and a clone because a clone will attempt to look exactly like what you see in the official product while a knockoff product will incorporate all of the unique features of the brand name product but come in at a lower price because they use lower quality material along with a not as popular brand. For instance, the most popular brand for Fitness tracking is currently Google but Samsung has developed a knock off product that is virtually the same thing for half the price. We don't normally think of Samsung as a knockoff product, but in this case it is.

Apple Machines

Apple has done something rather stupid and brilliant at the same time because they have decided to forgo repairing people's laptops in order to just junk the laptop for the source material inside. This has forced many of the Apple users of today, who want to recycle their old MacBooks or Apple computers, to donate the computers to the less fortunate. These types of computers are usually requested by students and the creative types who want to save money where their fellow colleagues have probably spent thousands. This is not to say that they are being cheap, but the common trend is that they don't want to spend money when they don't have to and righteously so.

The beauty about this is that they have created an artificial market increase, which means that the market doesn't necessarily need to be as expensive as it currently is but it is only as expensive as it currently is because of the company. An artificial increase normally happens because a company decides to forgo a decision that most people would find to be common sense. The decision here is that Apple will not recycle old devices to save consumers money.

However, that does not mean that consumers will readily allow Apple to gain a monopoly over their own product. Due to Apple making it more difficult to acquire repairs through Apple, this means that repair shops are finding that consumers are continuously knocking on their door in order to repair these devices because Apple won't do it for them. This means that when you take apart the Apple iPhone or

MacBook, almost every single part of that device will normally be sold on eBay if the device is relatively new. This means the device could have a cracked screen or the CPU could be blown, but, overall, the device has many working parts that can be sold separately to repair separate computers but it will be bought. This is unlike Android, which has a vast Market of products that can easily replace a good repair on a current Android phone.

This also brings us into another type of market, which is much smaller but much more effective in selling Apple laptops. You see, there are quite a few laptops made today that are compatible with the Mac OS, otherwise known as the operating system, which means that there are a number of laptops that can be turned into Macs. Since Apple users tend to be the pampered type of individual who don't know how to install an operating system onto their machine, they've always been able to just buy another machine if they don't know how to do it. This means, that so long as it has the Apple OS on the machine, they normally just care about whether it's fast or not. As I said though, this is a rather small market and is only geared for people who are looking to get a MacBook without getting a MacBook.

New Sells More In Every Country But Germany

While you could easily include Britain in this title, Germany has, by far, increased the number of used products that it buys. This could theoretically be explained by the large amount of people that invest in technology and DIY but most people just use this knowledge to their advantage. If you intend on selling used items, then the German Market is usually best for this but you have to be careful about shipping prices and what you're actually shipping because Germany is very strict on it consumer policies. On the other hand, if you were looking to sell something new then the best place to sell that would be Australia. This is thought to be because the island is rather disconnected from the rest of the world and most of the products that you find on the island are either products backed by companies that can afford to ship to Australia or products that are based in Australia. By the way, if you're trying to sell something that you could get a high return rate from then you may want to look at Australia when you go to sell that product.

HOW TO LIST ITEMS ON EBAY

List at The Beginning of the Week

If you plan on listing an item on eBay then the best time to start doing this is on a late Sunday because late Sunday is when everyone begins to lie down to go back to work. this also gives you the entire week and most of Saturday to sell to the General Public. However, Friday and Saturday will generally be the days where you will see the highest amount of sales because those are the days that the most amount of people will be sitting in front of the computer looking at eBay for products to buy.

Honest Description

Most customers can see through an overhyped description nowadays, because they've been exposed to it by so many companies over the past few decades. Having an honest description about your product will go a very long way towards securing a consumer base that trusts you. Having a consumer base that trusts you means that you will have a solid amount of people that will follow the products that you put out onto eBay and become regular purchasers.

Multiple Real Quality Photos

The average successful eBay listing has around 3 to 6 pictures of the actual product rather than pictures pulled off the internet. Just like the honest description, most customers can see through pictures that were taken off of a simple Google search. Having multiple quality photos of the product shows them that you are not trying to scam them.

Use Underscores In Your Title

When you create your title, you get about 54 characters before eBay cuts you off from whatever you put into the main page. This is all you get before your product title becomes a "..." at the end. A neat little trick that you can use in order to make your title take up two lines instead of the one line is to put underscores in your title. Underscores take up more pixel space and, by having two lines, you increase the overall amount of view area your product has the product listings. This will bring a lot more attention to your product over others.

Disclaimers for All

One of the things that you need to create whenever you decide that you want to be on eBay as a business rather than as a person, selling things as an occasional business is a disclaimer that covers you from being sued for promising different things. You can't always control a supplier, you can't always control the shipping that happens, and there are some things that are just out of your hands like the product being damaged while in route to the consumer. Having a disclaimer will save you from being sued for ridiculous reasons.

One Price Shipping and Paying

Most consumers will avoid anything that requires multiple complicated choices, which means that you need to figure out the average price of how much it's going to cost to ship a current item and then charge an overall amount for just shipping rather than having the different prices of the different shippers that you might use. This will bring everything into one choice and the consumer can just pay it without having to bother with trying to choose a shipping method.

Additionally, one of the things you want to do is try to set up as many pay options as you possibly can for the consumer, especially PayPal credit. Almost all transactions on eBay that occur regularly from regular customers will be through PayPal and PayPal credit. Without having PayPal credit on your account, you miss out on one of the largest spectrum of consumers that are out there for eBay sellers.

MAINTAINING A TOP RATED SELLER ACCOUNT

Honesty in All

This might come as a surprise to you if you have only ever thought of sellers on eBay to be trustworthy individuals provided they have a high rating. If you plan on making a business on eBay then you want to make sure that you are honest to a fault. The reason for this is because the more honest you are with a customer when explaining why a shipping issue is happening or why a current product may not be working for them the more likely they are to forgive you of any shortcomings that you might have in your business. Therefore, having as much honesty as you possibly can is one of the best ways to maintain a top-rated seller account.

Test As Many Products Sold As Possible

If you're a person who regularly shops on eBay for yourself then you will understand the frustration of getting a product that simply doesn't work and then getting a long list of troubleshooting methods that you already tried, which just proves that the person on the other end is not listening to you. It is always important to test the products that you sell to other people before you send the products out to them. The reason for this is because some products will work before they get to the customer and having a detailed account of a product that works before it gets to the customer can save you a lot of money with shipping because then you can hold the shipper accountable for the damages that were done and get a working product out the customer. Additionally, by testing the products that you sell you guarantee that the product is working and you can show the consumer that the product is working by simply recording the product test.

Be Realistic

You do not want to tell a customer that you're going to be able to give them 2-day shipping if you're not actually going to be able to give them 2-day shipping. One of the most frustrating things about businesses is that they will be late in sending out products and if you plan on being one of those individuals that has specific shipping days, then you don't want to advertise something like 2-day shipping or fast delivery because you can't guarantee that. You always want to be realistic with what you're selling your customer because the more realistic you are with them, the more that they will trust you and rate you even higher.

Being realistic can save you some hassle with customers that specifically go after eBay sellers to lower their top-rated selling stance. There are services out there that offer to bring down competitors in order to boost the sales of a new high rated seller on the platform. By being realistic with your customers, you can begin to understand how your general customers will react and be able to notice who is a fake and who is not. Regardless of what most people say about consumers, they tend to follow a pattern if they buy certain products from you.

Reliability is Best

One of the top qualities of nearly all high rated sellers on eBay is the reliability of that seller because most people don't want just another face that'll smile and tell you everything will be okay. What they want is a person who is a realist and who can be relied upon to do what they said they would do. While it may be a sad thing to hold people high for just being reliable, in the online world it is a rare commodity to have somebody that will contact you as soon as something goes wrong or provide you with vital information to get the order fixed. One of the hardest type of reviews to get is a recovery review because most sellers will lose their patience with the person on the other end simply because the person on the other end doesn't understand how the process works. However, getting a recovery review is often more beneficial to your status as a seller on eBay then a regular 5-star review is. This is because people care the most about how you will react as a business when something goes wrong on either end because most people don't want to buy from a business that will completely ignore them if something goes wrong. If you're buying something that's hundreds of dollars, you don't want a business that has a history of never getting back to the customer or being a general jerk whenever they have to deal with a customer. Instead, when you invest heavy amounts of money you want to hear about how awesome the seller is at making sure everything goes correctly and making sure everything that went incorrectly got fixed in the end in a smooth and easy manner.

Answer Questions

As odd as it may sound, you want to answer as many questions that pop up on your account as possible. Most people will judge a product by the questions that were answered because the product description is often seen as the part that is meant to sell the customer rather than inform the customer. Therefore, most people rely on the questions asked by previous buyers to determine whether they want to purchase the item or not. By making sure that you answer all the questions that your consumers might have about your product, you would ensure that you have the maximum amount of coverage needed to sell the product.

PICKING THE RIGHT PRICE

Choosing the right price for something can be either a task that's really easy or task that is so hard that many people hold onto a product until they can figure out what the right price should be. The honest truth is that there are four simple steps that you can follow to determine what the right price for your product will be. These steps have proven to work every time that I have put them into practice and other eBay sellers have put them into practice.

Choose Your Country

The first thing that you want to keep an eye on is the country that you plan on selling to because as I've mentioned before, many of the countries that you will be selling to have different price ranges for what they plan on buying. For instance, you know that you can usually price higher for used items in technology with Germany but you know that this isn't true for the United States because the entire market is saturated with the technology and used items. This is because there is a smaller population inside of Germany and having to overcome the barriers to sell to that country is something that most people don't want to tackle.

Ironically, the harder it is to get into a market the more profit can be made from a certain market. One thing that you do want to consider whenever you're selling to a different country is to make sure that you have the correct translations to everything because you may say something inappropriate or offensive if you just use something like Google Translate. While those things are useful for pronouncing certain things or figuring out what it actually says in your own language, they're not meant to be copied and pasted. Instead, you should often hire a ghostwriter that speaks that language to translate your material into the German version of that material.

With that said, you can normally determine the price tag by simply looking at the country itself and determining which products would sell better at a higher return rate. By doing this, not only do you get the higher amount of return right but you also make sure that the price that you give is not outlandish in comparison of what you expect the product to sell for. This is something that is hard for many new eBay sellers to wrap their head around, but there are some instances where the product seems like it's worth more but sells for much lower prices than other markets.

Low Stock Vs. High Stock

If there's a lot of high stock value in the market, then you want to sell along those prices but you also want to lower it in comparison to your competition. Depending on the market that you choose, you may find yourself in a situation where you are the one that prices the product and others follow you. This is a weird situation to be in because you are setting the prices for the day and while you may think that this is a bad thing, most of the time people will still purchase your product even though it is higher than that of what came out later. The reason for this is you maximize your payment options, which means that you may have employed the Buy It Now option. By employing this option, you give the person the ability to buy it immediately before anybody else can try to bid for it. While many people believe that the bulk of a sale comes from the ridiculous prices that you see on at auction house, the most common method of being paid regularly is by using the Buy It Now option. This is because you can set a dead price that covers all of what you need to cover along with what profit you would like to see from the product that you're selling.

Another issue you may encounter here is the fact that you may be in a market that suddenly went from high stock to low stock. This can normally happen over weeks and for certain periods of the year it may not be ideal to sell that certain type of product. For instance, most technology companies have a scheduled release date that's predictable and you don't want to be releasing out products during those times because people will be mostly focused on buying those products at those times period instead you want to hold on to the products that you have to see if what you are offering is currently a competing technology against what was released. A case in point is the Samsung Galaxy 7, which did absolutely horrible because it exploded in people's faces.

One of the top trends that occurred on nearly all selling platforms was that people would add humor to their product title by saying that the phone was not going to explode on them. This was a running joke that many people found amusing and this increased the amount of sales that occurred with phones that were Next Generation or previous to the Next Generation. This is why you always want to keep up-to-date on trends in the industry that you're selling in.

Compare Current Sales of Competitors

If you have ever sold a product before then you will understand that the first thing you do when selling to a market that already exists is to compare your prices and your quality to what your competitor has. This is because your competitor may have a product that is of a higher quality than you and selling at a certain price point, while another competitor may have something that's of a lower quality than you and selling at a certain price point that lower. This allows you to judge the exact amount that you need to use whenever you put your product on the market.

Additionally, you can begin to learn from your opponents by picking up on what they are all doing in the comments section, and what some of them are doing differently. You can tell what works by paying attention to the sellers that tend to sell more than everyone else by having up more products. This requires a little bit of investment of your time, but I guarantee you that it's well worth it.

Even Small Sales Are Some Sales

Something that I always found amazing about Amazon that not a lot of people understood was why people would be willing to sell their book for $0.99 rather than the $7 or $9 that a common paperback book would cost. The people who tend to ask these questions were usually the type of people who didn't understand that the author normally only made anywhere from $0.99 to $3 off of any given paperback book and the rest of the cost went to making the actual paperback. The truth of the matter is that regardless of how low the prices are, if you have a lot of something that is practically limitless, like an eBook, that you can sell for just a dollar in comparison to your competition that might be selling it for more than a dollar or much more than a dollar then it doesn't matter if you get 10,000 sales or a 100,000 sales just so long as you get sales. A book that sells 10,000 times at a dollar a piece will still earn you a profit of normally $10,000. Now, on a realistic scale, this isn't technically correct because Amazon does take some money out of it but with a place like eBay, where you are selling products like paperbacks and similar items that may not have an endless amount but have a lot of it, the principle still holds true. Essentially, as long as you make a profit in the sale it really only boils down to how many sales you make versus how much you make on each sale. You could easily sell 10 books for $10,000 to 10 customers or you could sell 1 million books for $1,000,000 to 1 million customers. Either way, you've made money and usually when you sell on a cheaper scale, you tend to have an easier time selling your product and other future products.

TIPS TO INCREASE YOUR EBAY PROFITS

Choose Your Country

Again, we're going to talk about which country you choose to sell in because you could easily be selling in the American Market where technology is oversaturated and very hard to sell in, or you could sell in the German Market where technology makes a significant amount more money. Making the choice to choose a specific country to sell to determines a great deal of how much you can make with that product. Remember, most of your transactions will be happening through PayPal so there will be an automatic conversion whenever you get paid through your eBay account most of the time. Therefore, it's almost always best to choose the country where your product tends to sell for a high return rate.

Additionally, you can easily search and find different surveys of people trying to figure out which markets sell better on eBay. There are market reports out there from tons of different companies over the years that will show you trends of what sells and what doesn't sell in certain countries and in certain other countries. Understanding this whole scheme of the selling tree will increase your eBay profits because you can then optimize your selling points to the markets that you need to sell to.

Stay In The Relative News

One of the key factors to making sure that you get paid a decent amount for the product that you're selling is to make sure that you stay up-to-date with the news of that industry. For example, if the new iPad were to come out tomorrow then it would be reasonable to expect nearly all of the older iPads to drop in price. By understanding when certain products are going to come out, you can do what's known as a Product Flush, which means that you sell all of your old items at a smaller profit margin to get rid of them before they become useless. Also, the companies that you may be selling products of may be selling products at a discounted price for a period of time. By keeping an eye out for this discounted price, you can skip telling certain products during certain times in order to maximize profit.

Create a Selling Network

Something that a lot of people who are new to selling on eBay don't understand is that many of the top-rated sellers actually have their own social networks for their business. This is because this gets their products out to the consumers who are used to buying from them. If a top-rated seller is known for being cheap, reliable, and quick about their sales then people will want to follow them for future sales. This means that these types of people are on YouTube, Twitter, and even Facebook most of the time in order to continuously promote their content. By creating a selling network, otherwise known as a social network, the business can usually find regular customers that will buy products from them on a consistent basis. Additionally, you can begin to sell exclusive material to customers who are interested in buying it. This means that you can normally get people to opt-in to subscription programs in order to buy items at a lower price than normal. This is kind of like the back channels of eBay and it occurs quite frequently amongst top rated sellers. One of the lucrative parts of these situations is that these consumers will often suggest other products that you want to obtain in order to sell to them. For instance, if you post something about a new product that you're selling like a smartphone oh, then you can look at the comments to see what they say you should be selling, like you should be selling this type of accessory with it.

Combo Deals

This actually brings me to my next point, which is how you can get into combo deals. Most people don't just buy a DSLR camera right off the bat and not buy a lens with it. There are certain products on the market that sell better if you provide a combo deal. The best part about this is that, most of the time, you can get combo deals up and going rather easily. For instance, you could sell a fire Kindle with an ornate design cover made only on Etsy that's been discontinued for a rather high price because most people will pay for that entire package. Another example is providing a carrying case for a DSLR camera for a price that seems lower than what retail would sell it for.

CONCLUSION

Selling on eBay is not as difficult as it may seem at first but it does require getting used to it and being patient with your consumers. You will not be a five-star highly rated seller within a few weeks of you joining eBay unless you're extremely lucky. In order to start your journey selling on eBay, if you're new, you need to begin to provide a product that is sustainable like small repair parts that are commonly bought. This will give you a good reputation that you need in order to get into bigger markets as you grow your business. It's always important to remember that you need to stay small in the beginning so that you can build out to a bigger better business later on. This is not going to be an instant process that makes you rich overnight, but a journey to see where you can sell the product in the best market.